In Art: New York City

{Enjoying Great Art Series}

Brought to you by

Catherine McGrew Jaime

Books in the "Enjoying Great Art" Series by Catherine Jaime:
- *In Art: Animals*
- *In Art: Books*
- *In Art: Bridges*
- *In Art: Candlelight*
- *In Art: Cats*
- *In Art: Christmas*
- *In Art: Eagles*
- *In Art: Food*
- *In Art: Hats*
- *In Art: Horses*
- *In Art: India*
- *In Art: Leonardo*
- *In Art: Lighthouses*
- *In Art: Maps & Globes*
- *In Art: Military*
- *In Art: Necklaces*
- *In Art: New York City*
- *In Art: Pastimes*
- *In Art: Self-Portraits*
- *In Art: Scions of Africa*
- *In Art: Shakespeare*
- *In Art: Trains*
- *In Art: Trees*
- *In Art: Turkey*
- *In Art: Parasols and Umbrellas*
- *In Art: U.S. Government*
- *In Art: U.S. States*
- *In Art: Venice*

Book in the series by Bonnie Hardison
- *In Art: Girls with Flowers*
- *In Art: Flowers*
- *In Art: Knights*

Books in the series by Deirdre Fuller:
- *In Art: America's National Parks*
- *In Art: Art*
- *In Art: Birds*
- *In Art: Butterflies*
- *In Art: Chairs*
- *In Art: Chickens*
- *In Art: Churches*
- *In Art: Clowns*
- *In Art: Dogs*
- *In Art: Donkeys*
- *In Art: Elephants*
- *In Art: Farming*
- *In Art: Pugs*
- *In Art: Sheep*
- *In Art: Shoes*
- *In Art: U.S. Presidents*
- *In Art: Winter*

Pictures used with Permission from the following Dover clip art books:

- *60 Great Travel Posters*
- *120 Great American Paintings*
- *120 Great Impressionist Paintings*
- *120 Great Paintings*
- *120 Great Travel Poster*
- *Old-Time American Cities and Sights*
- Vintage New York City Views

Copyright © 2014 by Catherine McGrew Jaime
www.CatherineJaime.com

Creative Learning Connection
8006 Old Madison Pike, Ste 11-A
Madison, AL 35758
www.CreativeLearningConnection.com

> *"One can't paint New York City as it is, but rather as it is felt."*
>
> Georgia O'Keeffe

When I think of cities in the United States, I think first of New York City – it has been a part of American history from before we became a country. But until recently I hadn't realized how many times it appeared in paintings through the centuries.

This small book takes a quick look at New York City through art. It is meant to be enjoyed by adults and students of all ages.

Look through these paintings that span many decades, and notice the similarities and the differences between them…See the colors, the textures and patterns, and more. Take note of whether there are people included in the different paintings; and if so, are men, women, or children more often portrayed? Do you like certain artists or styles more than others?

But, most of all, enjoy!

The Battery and Harbor

Thomas Birch, 1811

New York from the Steeple of Saint Paul's Church Looking East, South, and West

Henry Papprill, 1848

Broadway at Spring Street

Hippolyte Sebron, 1855

Wall Street, Half Past Two O'Clock, October 13, 1857

James Cafferty and Charles G. Rosenberg, 1858

New York Harbor and Battery

Andrew Melrose, 1885

Statue of Liberty Enlightening the World

Edward P. Moran, 1886

The New York Yacht Club Regatta

Charles Parsons and Lyman Atwater, 1869

Fifth Avenue at Washington Square

Childe Hassam, 1891

A Winter Wedding – Washington Square

Fernand Lungreen, 1897

Above: Fruit Stand Coney Island

Below: Washington Square Park

William Glackens, 1898 & 1908

New York Harbor

George Herbert McCord, c.1899

Street Scene with Snow (57th Street)

Robert Henri, 1902

Above: Morningside Heights

Below: The Flatiron Building

Both: Ernest Lawson, 1902 - 1905

Battery Park

William Glackens, 1902 - 1904

Street Scene (Hester Street)

George Luks, 1905

Old Grand Central Station

Colin Campbell Cooper, 1906

Rainy Day, Madison Square

Paul Cornoyer, 1907 – 1908

Flat Iron Building

Colin Campbell Cooper, 1908

Pennsylvania Station Excavation

George Wesley Bellows, c.1908

Above: Woolworth Bridge Under Construction

Below: Brooklyn Bridge

Both: John Marin, 1911 & 1912

Lower New York

Edward Redfield, 1910

Six O'Clock

John Sloan, 1912

Along the River Front, New York

Everett Longley Warner, 1912

Italo-American Celebration, Washington Square

William Glackens, 1912

Spring Night, Harlem River

Ernest Lawson, 1913

Cliff Dwellers (Lower East Side)

George Bellows, 1913

Backyards, Greenwich Village

John Sloan, 1914

Lower Broadway in Wartime

Colin Campbell Cooper, 1917

Jefferson Market, Sixth Avenue

John Sloan, 1917

The Brooklyn Bridge

Joseph Stella, 1922

New York Restaurant

Edward Hopper, 1922

Skyscrapers

Charles Sheeler, 1922

The City from Greenwich Village

John Sloan, 1922

Central Park

Colin Campbell Cooper, 1927 – 1931

East River from the 30th Story of the Shelton Hotel

Georgia O'Keeffe, 1928

New York Central Building

Chesley Bonestell, 1930

www.ingramcontent.com/pod-product-compliance
Lightning Source LLC
Chambersburg PA
CBHW040753200526
45159CB00025B/2081